P9-CEH-522

3 1163 00092 6526

12/11/96

PRINCESS OF THE PRESS

Books by Angela Shelf Medearis

Rainbow Biographies
Dare to Dream:
Coretta Scott King and the Civil Rights Movement
Little Louis and the Jazz Band:
The Story of Louis "Satchmo" Armstrong

The Freedom Riddle

Annie's Gifts
Big Mama and Grandma Ghana
Bye, Bye Babies
The Spray Paint Mystery
Come This Far to Freedom
Dancing with the Indians
Eat Babies Eat
Harry's House
Haunts: Tales from African-American Folklore
Here Comes the Snow
The 100th Day of School
Our People
Picking Peas for a Penny
Poppa's New Pants
The Seven Days of Kwanzaa
The Singing Man
Skin Deep and Other Teenaged Reflections
The Adventures of Sugar and Junior
Tailypo
Too Much Talk
Treemonisha
We Eat Dinner in the Bathtub
We Play on a Rainy Day
The Zebra-Riding Cowboy

The African-American Kitchen Cookbook (adult)
The Kwanzaa Celebration Cookbook (adult)

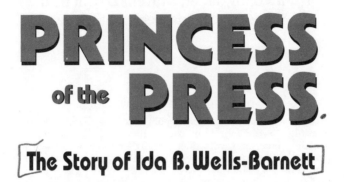

PRINCESS of the PRESS.

The Story of Ida B. Wells-Barnett

ANGELA SHELF MEDEARIS

A RAINBOW BIOGRAPHY

LODESTAR BOOKS
Dutton   New York

To my baby sister, Marcia D. Shelf, the
Princess of Business, with love
A.S.M.

Library of Congress Cataloging-in-Publication Data

Medearis, Angela Shelf, 1956–
   Princess of the press: the story of Ida B. Wells-Barnett / Angela
Shelf Medearis.—1st ed.
      p.   cm.—(A Rainbow biography)
   Includes bibliographical references and index.
   Summary: A biography of the journalist, newspaper owner, and
suffragette who campaigned for civil rights and founded the
National Association for the Advancement of Colored People.
   ISBN 0-525-67493-4 (alk. paper)
   1. Wells-Barnett, Ida B., 1862–1931—Juvenile literature.
2. Afro-American women civil rights workers—Biography—
Juvenile literature.   3. Civil rights workers—United States—
Biography—Juvenile literature.   4. Journalists—United
States—Biography—Juvenile literature.   5. United States—Race
relations—Juvenile literature.   [1. Wells-Barnett, Ida B.,
1862–1931.   2. Civil rights workers.   3. Journalists.   4. Race
relations.   5. Afro-Americans—Biography.   6. Women—
Biography.]   I. Title.   II. Series.
E185.97.W55M43   1997
323'.092—dc21   [B]   97-8520   CIP   AC

Published in the United States by Lodestar Books,
an affiliate of Dutton Children's Books,
a member of Penguin Putnam Inc.,
375 Hudson Street, New York, New York 10014

Published simultaneously in Canada
by McClelland & Stewart, Toronto

Editor: Rosemary Brosnan   Designer: Marilyn Granald

Printed in the U.S.A.
First Edition
2 4 6 8 10 9 7 5 3 1

Contents

A Letter From Home

On a cool fall day in 1876, Ida Bell Wells scrubbed the pans left from the morning dishes. She was paying a visit to her grandmother Wells's farm, and had only recently recovered from a bout of chills and fever. Ida was still feeling a little ill, and she was also homesick. She missed her parents and her little brothers and sisters. Her mother, Lizzie, was one of the best cooks in the county. Her father, Jim, was a wonderful carpenter and shared Ida's love for reading the news and also enjoyed hearing Ida read aloud. Jim was also active in the Republican party and often discussed the power of the vote and current events with Ida.[1]

Ida's brother Jim Jr. was eleven, George was nine, and chubby little Stanley, her baby brother, was nine months old. Another brother, Eddie, had died of spinal meningitis when Ida was a little girl. Her sister, Eugenia, who was eleven, had been physically disabled for the last seven years with a disease that left her spine twisted and her legs without feeling.

Although Eugenia was often ill and unable to walk, she was one of Ida's closest friends and play-mates. Ida also wondered what her pesky little sis-ters, five-year-old Annie and two-year-old Lillie, were doing. Ida was fourteen and the oldest, so she often helped her parents take care of her younger brothers and sisters. She missed the noise and the laughter that filled their house in Holly Springs, Mississippi. Ida's parents worked hard to make sure all of their children were loved and cared for. They wanted them to have a better life than their own.[2]

Both of Ida's parents had been born into slavery. Jim's father was a slave owner who had purchased Jim's mother, Peggy. Jim was his only son. Master Wells would not allow Jim to be mistreated and made sure he had a good education. As soon as he turned eighteen, Jim was apprenticed to Mr. Bolling, a local carpenter, so that he could learn a skill. Ida's mother, Lizzie, was Mr. Bollings's cook. Jim and Lizzie fell in love, and a slave marriage was performed.

Unlike Ida's father, her mother had been cruelly treated as a slave. When they were children, Lizzie and her sister, Belle, were separated from their family and sold from one mean owner to the next. Lizzie spent her life trying to locate the rest of her family without success.[3]

The Civil War started in 1861. In 1863, President Abraham Lincoln issued the Emancipation Procla-mation, which freed the slaves in the Confederate states. Ida was six months old. By 1865, the North had defeated the South, and slavery came to an end everywhere in America. The Southern states started to rebuild, and a period called Reconstruction began. During this time, African-American men had the right to vote, and African-Americans could start their own businesses. Jim and Lizzie remarried as a free man and woman, determined to build a good life for themselves and for their family.

The Freedmen's Aid Society started a school for the newly freed slaves—Shaw University. Like many former slaves who had been denied the chance to learn, Jim and Lizzie valued education. Jim became a trustee at the university, and Ida was one of the first children to attend the school. Ida excelled in all her classes, and was far ahead of the other students. Lizzie attended classes at Shaw University five days a week, along with Ida and the rest of the children. She had never learned to read or write because it was against the law for slaves to be educated. One of Lizzie's proudest moments was when she was finally able to read the Bible by herself.

Saturdays were a busy time at the Wells's house. Ida spent the day helping her mother with the cleaning. Her father and brother made sure everyone's shoes were polished. Lizzie and Ida pressed clothes, bathed the younger children, and washed their hair. Ida helped her mother prepare Sunday dinner so that it would be ready for them to eat after church. Every Sunday morning, the Wells family sat on a wooden pew side by side. Once, the Wellses received the prize for perfect attendance for a year.[4]

Ida sighed as she dried the dishes. At first, she had been looking forward to visiting her grand-mother. She thought it would be fun to leave her regular chores and her baby-sitting duties and get away for awhile. Now she wished she was back at home. A few days after Ida arrived at her grand-mother's house, she received the news that a horrible epidemic of yellow fever was sweeping through Memphis, Tennessee, which was about fifty miles away from Holly Springs. The mayor of Holly Springs had refused to quarantine the town, and the fever had spread there. This same disease had killed many people three years earlier. Ida hoped that her family had left town and escaped the sickness, but she wasn't sure. The mail didn't come very often to Grandmother Wells's farm, and Ida hadn't heard from her family in several days.

As Ida stacked the dishes in the cabinet, she heard a knock at the front door. She smiled when she recognized three men who were friends of her parents. The men sat down in the living room and looked solemnly at Ida. One of them handed her a letter. It was from Ida's next-door neighbor. Ida hoped that the letter would contain some news about her family.

As Ida quickly read the first page, she grew more and more frightened. Many people had died from the yellow fever that had swept through the town, and hundreds were sick. As Ida turned the page, one terrible paragraph leapt out at her: "Jim and Lizzie Wells both died of yellow fever within twenty-four hours of each other. The children are all at home and the Howard Association has put a woman there to take care of them. Send word to Ida."[5]

Ida couldn't believe that her parents were dead. She sat numbly for what seemed like hours. Her grandmother, who had been joined by her aunt and uncle, tried to comfort her, but Ida didn't respond to what they were saying. She was worried about her younger brothers and sisters and wondered how they were doing. She knew that the woman from the Howard Association would take good care of them until she arrived.

The Howard Association was a charity of which her father had been a member. The association took care of the sick and orphaned.

In order to stop the spread of yellow fever, Ida's parents would be buried immediately. Ida would not be able to attend the funeral. She was heartbroken.

Like many young women of her time, Ida kept a diary. Her diary was like a good friend, a place she could write down her thoughts, hopes, and fears. It made Ida feel better to write down everything that was happening to her. "I wanted to go home at once," Ida wrote in her diary after learning about her parents' deaths. "But not until three days later, on the receipt of a letter from the doctor in charge [from the Howard Association], who said I ought to come home, were they willing to let me go." She continued:

> When my uncle and I got to the next railroad town, from which I was to take the train to Holly Springs, all the people in that station urged me not to go. They were sure that coming from the country I would fall victim [to the fever] at once, and that it was better for me to stay away until the epidemic was over, so that I could take care of the children, if any were left. . . . I consented to stay there and write home. But when I thought of my crippled sister [Eugenia], of the smaller children all down to my nine-month-old baby brother, the conviction grew within me that I ought to be with them.[6]

Ida went back to the railroad station, determined to return home. Because of the yellow fever, no passenger trains were available, so Ida paid to ride on a freight train that normally hauled cargo and animals. The train was draped with black cloth, because two of the conductors had recently died from yellow fever. The remaining conductor told Ida she was making a mistake and that she should stay in the country.

"Why are you running the train when you know you will probably get the fever?" Ida asked the conductor.

"Someone has to do it," he replied.

"That's exactly why I am going home," Ida told him. "I am the oldest of seven children. There's nobody but me to look after them now. Don't you think I should do my duty too?" The conductor didn't say anything else, but Ida knew that he thought she would probably catch the fever and die. When the train reached Holly Springs, he waved good-bye to Ida as though he would never see her again.[7]

We Will Not Be Separated

When Ida finally arrived at her home, she found out that Stanley, her baby brother, had died from the fever, and that all of the children, except her sister Eugenia, were sick. The family doctor scolded Ida and told her that she shouldn't have come home, but Eugenia was happy to see her.

"When the fever first broke out, we couldn't leave because there was no room for us at Aunt Belle's house," Eugenia told Ida. "Father went about his work, nursing the sick and making coffins for the dead. He sent us food and money, but he would not come home at night for fear of spreading the sickness to us. Then Mother got the fever, and Father came to help nurse her. He came down with the fever, too, and died the day before she did."[1]

Eugenia began to cry. Ida put her arms around her sister and hugged her tightly.

"Everything will be all right," Ida said. "I'm home now."

The next day, Ida began to feel ill and trembled

with chills and fever. The nurse who was tending to the other children also took care of Ida. Ida was ill for four days, but slowly she began to recover. As soon as she felt strong enough, Ida went into town to take care of the family business.

After their father died, Eugenia had given Doctor Gray, who was assigned to the family from the Howard Association, three hundred dollars to lock in a safe. Eugenia knew that Dr. Gray would be leaving town soon, and she was anxious to get the money from him before he left. Eugenia wrote Dr. Gray a note and gave it, along with the receipt for the money, to Ida to deliver to him.

The town was crowded with people, and Ida wasn't sure who Dr. Gray was. She asked someone to point him out to her. When she told Dr. Gray who she was he smiled.

"So you are Genie's big sister," Dr. Gray said. "Tell her the treasurer has the key to the safe, and he is out in the country to see his family. He will be back this evening, and I will bring her the money tonight, as I am leaving tomorrow. You children had a wonderful father. He was one of the best aides in helping us with the sick. He'd be passing through the courthouse on his way to the shop; if a patient was restless, he would stop to quiet him, if he were dying he would talk to him or pray with him, then pick up his tools and go on with the rest of the day's work. Everyone liked him, and we all missed him when he was gone."[2]

Ida smiled and thanked him. The three hundred

dollars would not go very far, but it would help buy food, medicine, and clothing for her family until Ida could think of a way to take care of them all.

As soon as the yellow fever epidemic was over, a meeting was scheduled to discuss the children's future. That evening, Ida hurriedly gave her little sisters a bath and put them to bed. Then she helped Eugenia get comfortable for the night. The two boys weren't ready to go to sleep yet, so Ida allowed them to sit out on the front steps. Ida could hear the boys talking quietly to each other. Then she waited for her father's friends to arrive for the meeting.

Ida's father had belonged to a group called the Masons, a charitable brotherhood that took care of the needs of its members. The Masons wanted to help and protect Ida and her brothers and sisters. After everyone had arrived, the men talked among themselves about what should be done with the children. They discussed each child almost as if Ida weren't there.

"We've always wanted a young'un of our own," Brother Gresham said. "The Lord never blessed us, so we would love to have little Lillie. She is only two, and we could raise her as our own."

"And Annie is just about the age of our Dorothy and would be right smart company for her," Brother Dobbs said. "Martha and I will take Annie."

"Jim and George can go with Henry Allen," Brother Miller said. "He is a carpenter, too, and has said he will give the boys a home. Jim is eleven now and can drive a nail straight as his daddy used to.

George is almost as good, even though he is only nine. You know, Big Jim spent lots of time teaching them, and nobody could have put up a better fence than that one outside, and many a grown man couldn't have done as well."

The Wellses' house was small and neat, and a picket fence surrounded a lovely flower bed that had been the pride and joy of Ida's mother.

"Poor Eugenia," Brother Hall said. "What can we do about Eugenia? She can't do nothing but sit in her chair all day. Everybody I talked to said it was best to send her to the poorhouse. They can care for her there better than anywhere else, and her so sickly too."

No one came up with a better solution or offered Eugenia a home, so the men nodded in agreement. She would be sent to the poorhouse, a place for homeless women and children.

"Ida, you're old enough to find a job," Brother Miller said. "You're fourteen now, and you should be able to find work tending white folks' children. I'm sure someone will hire you and give you a home."

"If we sell this house, it will bring in a nice amount of money," said Brother Hall. "We can put that money along with the money you'll receive from your parents' death benefit into a trust fund. Brother Miller and I will be your guardians and look after things for you."

As Ida listened to the men talk, she grew more and more furious. During that time, children were taught by their elders to be "seen but not heard." They were told that it was bad manners to question the decisions made by adults. The men were shocked when Ida rose to her feet and interrupted the meeting.

"I've been listening to all you have had to say and I can't let you do it," Ida said calmly. "My mama and papa would turn over in their graves if they knew their children were scattered all over Holly Springs. And I can't bear the thought of Eugenia in a poorhouse. We will not be separated. If you help me find a job, I will work and take care of us."

The men stared at Ida as she walked outside and told Jim Jr. and George that it was time for bed. She knew they had been listening to the meeting and were probably worried.

"Ida," Jim Jr. whispered. "What's going to happen to us?"

"I'm going to keep you all right here at home and find work to do," Ida said. "The Masons are going to help me, and all of you will have to help too. Now go to bed. Everything's going to work out fine."

The boys hurried off to bed, and Ida returned to the meeting. The men were whispering among themselves. When they noticed Ida had come back, they stopped talking. Brother Miller rose to his feet.

"You've always done well in school, Ida," Brother Miller said. "Perhaps you can take the teaching certification examination and get a job as a school teacher. If you think you can take care of your family, then we'll do our best to help you."

Ida smiled. She hadn't thought of becoming a teacher, but she had always been a good student.

"Then it's settled," Ida said. "We have enough money to last us for a little while. We'll be all right until I can find a teaching position."

"Who will take care of the children while you're teaching?" Brother Hall asked.

"Granny Wells will come from the country if I ask her," Ida said.

"I'll send Sister Miller over to help you tomorrow," Brother Miller said. "We'll see how things go and take it from there."[3]

Ida thanked the men and got ready for bed. She hid her worries about the future from her father's friends and the other children, but she was honest about her fears in her diary.

"After being a happy, light-hearted school girl," Ida wrote, "I suddenly found myself at the head of a family."[4]

New Beginnings

The next morning, while Ida made breakfast, the other children crowded around Eugenia's chair. Eugenia made sure all the children's faces were clean, their teeth were brushed, and their clothes were buttoned. She combed Annie's and Lillie's hair and watched over them as they played.

"If everyone works hard, we can keep our home together," Ida said. "I'm going to try to get Grandmother to live with us."

"There's not much I can do, is there?" Eugenia said sadly.

"Yes, as much as you've always done," Ida said. "You've been the biggest help in the world. You just keep looking after Annie and Lillie. You'll be good girls and do what Genie tells you to do, won't you?" Ida asked the two little girls.

"I always do what Genie says, don't I, Genie?" Annie said. "And I make Lillie mind too."

Ida smiled at her brothers and sisters. For the

first time in days she felt that things were going to get better.

Later that afternoon, Sister Miller and a few other women from the neighborhood came to help Ida. Although everyone felt that Ida would probably score high on the teacher's examination, in order to get a teaching job, she would have to look much older than fourteen. Sister Miller decided that what Ida needed was a new hairstyle.

After Sister Miller finished, she led Ida to the mirror. Ida barely recognized herself. Her long, thick black braids and pink hair bows were gone. The young lady who stared back at Ida from the mirror had her hair piled on top of her head in a neat bun.

"You know, child," Sister Miller said as she looked her over from head to toe, "young ladies wear their dresses below their shoe tops. Since you're going to play at being a young lady, you'll have to dress like one."

The women took Lizzie's dresses and cut and sewed them to fit Ida. The skirts of Ida's new dresses were so long, they trailed behind her on the floor. Ida had to practice walking so that she wouldn't trip and fall over the long skirts.[1]

That afternoon, Ida went down to the school board and took the teacher's examination. She passed and was hired to teach at a school six miles out in the country for twenty-five dollars a month. Grandmother Wells left her farm and stayed with the younger children while Ida was at work. Although she was seventy years old, Grandmother Wells was determined to help support her grandchildren. She took a job as a maid during the day, while Eugenia watched over Lillie and Annie and the boys attended school. Every evening, Grandmother Wells cleaned the house and cared for Ida's younger brothers and sisters.

From Monday through Friday, Ida lived with the Lewis family and taught in a run-down, one-room country schoolhouse. The little schoolhouse was at the intersection of two dirt roads in northern Mississippi. Ida's students sat on rough wooden benches. They had very few books or materials to write with and the walls were bare, but Ida's class was eager to learn. Ida taught everyone from young children to adults. The book most of the adults wanted to learn to read was the Bible.

As time went by, Ida became known as a very good teacher. Although Ida's students were often older than she was, they still called her "Miss Ida" and treated her with respect. Every Friday, just before Ida made the long six-mile journey home, her students showered her with gifts. Eggs, syrup, butter, and fresh vegetables were piled on the back of Ida's slow-moving mule, Ginger.

Ida's students walked with her up the road as she tried to get Ginger to trot, but she couldn't get the plump mule to move faster. At the turn in the road, the students waved good-bye to Ida and went their separate ways.

When Ida finally arrived home, Grandmother and her sisters and brothers eagerly questioned her.

"How was work, daughter?" Grandmother Wells asked. "Did everyone come to school this week?"

"What did you bring us?" her sisters and brothers asked.

"Wait, wait, one at a time!" Ida said. She showed everyone the food her students had given her and told them about her week.

"Old Ginger is getting fatter every day," Ida said as the boys led the mule away. "They keep him the whole week for me and all he has to do is eat. I told them to put him to work with their mule or he will be so fat he can't walk!"[2]

Grandmother and Ida spent all day Saturday cooking, cleaning, mending, and scrubbing. The boys shined everyone's shoes for church, and Eugenia combed Lillie's and Annie's hair. The Wells family still attended church every Sunday morning just as they had done when Jim and Lizzie were alive. On Sunday evenings, Ida would mount Ginger and ride back to the Lewises' home in the country to get ready for another week of teaching.

One evening, while Ida was away at school, Grandmother Wells suffered a stroke that paralyzed part of her body. She could no longer care for herself or the children. Ida's Aunt Belle took Grandmother Wells back to the farm to care for her. To keep her family together, Ida needed someone to watch over the children. She found a woman who had been an old friend of her mother's to

17

stay at the house until Ida finished the school term.

Ida's Aunt Fannie, who lived in Memphis, arranged for Ida to live with her and teach at another country school in Woodstock, Tennessee. Her Aunt Belle, her mother's sister, offered to care for Eugenia, as well as Jim Jr. and George. Her brothers were old enough to be apprenticed as carpenters and were eager to learn the trade. They also helped Aunt Belle on her farm. Eugenia had become weaker and required more care and attention. Ida hated to leave her brothers and sister behind, but she felt that it was best for everyone. She took Lillie and Annie with her to Memphis to start a new life.

Although Ida's new teaching job provided her with a better salary, it was so far from Memphis that she had to ride the train to visit her family on the weekends. Every day after school, Ida studied for the Memphis Teachers' Examination. If she passed the test, she would be able to work in Memphis and would be closer to Annie and Lillie.

On May 4, 1884, Ida boarded a train to return to school in Woodstock after visiting her family. Whites and blacks paid the same price for a train ticket, but they did not receive equal accommodations or treatment. Since the end of the Civil War, many whites had found ways to take away the rights and freedoms that African-Americans had gained when slavery came to an end.

Slowly, more and more laws were being passed in the South that separated whites from blacks in public schools, restaurants, housing, and trans-

18

portation. The Civil Rights Bill of 1866, which had been ratified to guarantee the rights of African-Americans, was declared unconstitutional by the United States Supreme Court in 1883. At the time Ida bought her ticket, the law stated that accommodations must be separate but equal for white and black passengers. However, white passengers rode in a clean rail car, while blacks and smokers were forced to ride in dirty, crowded cars.

When the conductor came around to collect the tickets, he refused to accept Ida's first-class pass. Ida felt that if he didn't want her ticket she wouldn't be bothered about it and continued reading her book. When the conductor finished collecting all of the tickets, he returned to Ida's seat. He told her that she would have to sit in the smoking car. Ida refused to move.

The conductor demanded that Ida move immediately. He grabbed her arm to pull her out of the seat. Although she was very small, Ida was not at all afraid of the conductor. She sank her teeth into his hand. The conductor howled in pain and left to find someone to help him remove Ida from the train. Ida braced herself by holding onto the seat in front of her and pushing her feet against the floor. If the conductor was going to try to move her, she wasn't going to make it easy for him. The conductor enlisted the help of the baggage man and another man. Together, they dragged Ida out of her seat. Ida wrote about the incident in her diary:

[O]f course they succeeded in dragging me out. They were encouraged to do this by the attitude of the white ladies and gentlemen in the car; some of them even stood on the seats so that they could get a good view and continued applauding the conductor for his brave stand.

By this time, the train had stopped at the first station. When I saw that they were determined to drag me into the smoker, which was already filled with colored people and those who were smoking, I said I would get off the train rather than go in—which I did. Strangely, I held onto my ticket all this time, and although the sleeves of my linen duster had been torn out and I had been pretty roughly handled, I had not been hurt physically.[3]

Ida decided to fight back. She hired a lawyer to take her case to court. After her lawyer began delaying the case, and months went by, Ida discovered that the railroad had paid him to work on its side against her. Ida fired him and hired Judge Greer, who worked to bring the case to state court. The railroad approached Ida and offered her money to drop the case. Ida refused. She didn't want money—she wanted the right to be treated like any other human being. Ida's decision to fight against this injustice changed her life.

Iola, Princess of the Press

On December 25, 1884, the Memphis *Daily Appeal* carried this headline in bold print: **"A Darky Damsel Obtains a Verdict for Damages Against the Chesapeake and Ohio Railroad—What It Cost To Put a Colored Teacher in a Smoking Car—Verdict for $500!"**[1]

Ida had won her case and been awarded five hundred dollars, but the railroad wasn't through fighting her. The owners of the railroad appealed the case to the Tennessee Supreme Court and another judge. The owners were afraid that Ida's case would give African-Americans rights under the law that they'd lost when the Civil Rights Bill was repealed. They felt they couldn't afford to have Ida's case help bring about a more equal system under the law for whites and blacks. The railroad was also afraid others would sue.

The Tennessee Supreme Court reversed the findings of the lower court and took away both Ida's victory and her money. Because she lost the case in the

Supreme Court, Ida was forced to pay two hundred dollars in damages.

By the time the case was settled, Ida had found a better-paying teaching job in Memphis, so she no longer had to travel back and forth on the train. Ida loved living in Memphis. She was twenty-five years old, and for the first time she was living in a big city. Although Ida accepted offers to teach in other states, she would always return to Memphis after a few weeks.

Unlike other young women of her time, Ida felt no real urgency to be married because she had cared for her brothers and sisters since she was a child. Ida enjoyed her life as a single young woman. For the first time, she was not responsible for anyone but herself. Her brothers, Jim Jr. and George, were both working as carpenters. Lillie and Annie had recently moved to California with their aunt Fannie. Death had taken Eugenia and Grandmother Wells within a short time of each other. Ida lived alone in various rooming houses around the city.

Ida was fond of having a male companion and had fallen in love once or twice while living in Memphis. But she hated the way that women of her time were expected to behave. "I will not begin at this late day by doing that that my soul abhors," Ida wrote in her diary, "sugaring men, weak, deceitful creatures, with flattery to retain them as escorts or to gratify a revenge."[2]

Ida was always torn between patterning herself after the quietly reserved, restrained way women of the 1800s were supposed to behave, and being true to her real self—the bold, ambitious, no-nonsense, intellectually curious, and outspoken person that she really was. This behavior was considered unladylike and masculine during the late nineteenth century.

Ida was an interesting and complicated person. She was vain and loved having her picture taken. Ida also had a passion for shopping. In her diary, she often described how she had spent too much money on a pretty dress, a hat, or pair of gloves. In her beautifully tailored clothes, she walked as if she owned the world.

Ida had many interests, including attending the large African-American churches in Memphis to hear the sermons; going horseback riding; watching baseball games; attending concerts and plays; participating in lively conversations; playing checkers and Parcheesi; and traveling. She attended summer sessions at Fisk University in Nashville, Tennessee, and enjoyed learning and debating about every aspect of a topic.

Ida also loved to read. She wrote in her diary that "I had formed my ideals on the best of [Charles] Dickens's stories, Louisa May Alcott's, Mrs. A. D. T. Whitney's and Charlotte Bronte's books, and Oliver Optic's stories for boys. I had read the Bible and Shakespeare through, but I had never read a Negro book or anything about Negroes."[3] Her detailed diary and journal entries are evidence that she enjoyed writing as well.

Ida was a member of a literary club that met every Friday afternoon. The young men and women, most of whom were teachers, enjoyed quoting from their favorite books, making speeches, reading essays they had written, and listening to music. At the end of each meeting, they read aloud from a newspaper called the *Evening Star*. Ida described the paper as "a spicy journal." Owned and written by African-Americans, it offered its readers thought-provoking news and opinions. When the editor of the *Evening Star* moved to Washington, D.C., Ida was chosen to take his place. "I tried to make my offering as acceptable as his had been," Ida wrote in her diary, "and before long I found that I liked the work."[4] Ida enjoyed writing items for the paper and reading them aloud at the Friday afternoon meetings.

Other newspapers began reprinting Ida's articles, and she received an offer to write for a paper published by the Baptist church called *The Living Way*. Ida's first article for *The Living Way* was a detailed account of her court case against the railroad. African-American newspapers around the United States reprinted the article.

Ida believed that her articles should tell a reader the truth in a simple, no-nonsense way. She signed her work "Iola," and African-American newspapers in other states regularly reprinted her pieces and asked her to write new articles for them. She was elected secretary of the Colored Press Association in 1889. The National Press Association called Ida "the princess of the press."

Although she was still working as a teacher, writing became more and more appealing to Ida. "I had made a reputation in school for thoroughness and discipline in the primary grades," Ida noted in her diary, "[but] I was never promoted above the fourth grade in all my years as a teacher. The confinement and monotony of the primary work began to grow distasteful. The correspondence I had built up in newspaper work gave me an outlet through which to express the real 'me,' and I enjoyed my work to the utmost."[5]

When Ida was twenty-seven years old, she was offered the opportunity to write for the *Memphis Free Speech and Headlight,* which was owned by J. L. Fleming and Reverend Taylor Nightingale, pastor of one of the largest African-American churches in town. "I refused to come in except as equal with themselves, and I bought a one-third interest," Ida wrote. "I was editor, Mr. Fleming was business manager, and Rev. Nightingale was sales manager."[6]

Ida continued teaching during the day to pay for the newspaper and to support herself. She spent her nights and weekends at the newspaper. She decided that something needed to be done to improve the poor condition of the school buildings for African-Americans and the outdated books and materials black children had to use at school. She wrote an article about the schools that also criticized the qualifications of some of the African-American teachers.

"Needless to say," Ida wrote later, "that article created a sensation and much comment." Because of what she had written, Ida lost her teaching position. "But I thought it was right to strike a blow against a glaring evil and I did not regret it."[7]

Ida was determined to make a living as a writer. She began traveling around the country to introduce people to her newspaper and to urge them to subscribe. "In nine months," Ida wrote, "I had an income as nearly as large as I had received teaching and felt sure that I had found my vocation. I was very proud of my success because up to that time very few of our newspapers had made any money."[8]

Ida purchased Reverend Nightingale's share of the paper and became co-owner with J. L. Fleming. Then she began printing the newspaper on pink paper so that it stood out from other newspapers.

In March 1892, Ida sadly noted in her diary that "while I was thus carrying on the work of my newspaper, happy in the thought that our influence was helpful and I was doing the work I loved and had proved I could make a living out of it, there came the lynching in Memphis which changed the whole course of my life."[9]

A lynching occurs when an angry mob kills a person without due process of law. Since the beginning of the American slave trade in the eighteenth century, hundreds of African-American men, women, and children had been lynched by being hanged from the neck, burned alive, or shot. Although Ida knew that lynchings happened fairly often in the South, she had felt that the person who was lynched had done something wrong to deserve such a horrible punishment. The incident that became known as "the lynching at the Curve" affected her deeply and changed her views about lynching forever.

Thomas Moss and his wife, Betty, were two of Ida's closest friends. She was godmother to their

Ida with her friend Betty Moss, the widow of Thomas Moss, and Betty's children, Thomas Jr. and Maurine. Ida was Maurine's godmother. Thomas Moss was lynched by a mob in 1892. DEPARTMENT OF SPECIAL COLLECTIONS, THE UNIVERSITY OF CHICAGO LIBRARY

daughter, Maurine. Thomas was a mail carrier who visited Ida's newspaper offices every day with letters and the latest news around town. Moss, along with Calvin McDowell and Henry Stewart, owned a business they called the People's Grocery Company in an area of Memphis known as "the Curve," because the streetcar tracks curved sharply at that point.

For a long time, a white grocery store had received most of the business in that area. When Thomas Moss and his partners opened their store, they began attracting many of the shoppers. Their business blossomed and their success made the other storekeeper jealous and angry. An argument at the Curve between a group of children, some white and some black, erupted into threats to "clean out the People's Grocery Company."

Moss and his partners consulted a lawyer who told them that they would not receive police protection because they were outside of the city limits. He advised them to arm themselves and protect their property. That night, March 5, 1892, around ten o'clock, three white men broke into the back of the People's Grocery Company and were shot and wounded.

The white-owned newspapers in Memphis ran several untrue stories claiming that the men who broke into the store were officers of the law, and that they were "hunting up criminals whom they had been told were harbored in the People's Grocery Company . . . a resort of thieves and thugs."[10]

The Memphis police used the incident as an

excuse to raid the homes of more than one hundred African-American men and arrest and jail them on charges of "suspicion." Some white men were allowed inside the jail to point out the owners of the People's Grocery Company. Fearing trouble, several black men in Memphis armed themselves and stood outside the jail to prevent any lynchings. After a couple of days, the men believed that the tension had eased and the crisis had passed, so they stopped standing guard at the jail.

That very night, the guards let a mob of white men into the jail. They yanked Thomas Moss, Calvin McDowell, and Henry Stewart out of their cells and took them outside the city limits to Cubbins Brick Yard. An eyewitness account said that Thomas Moss "begged for his life for the sake of his wife and child and his unborn baby." When asked if he had any last words, Moss said "tell my people to go West—there is no justice for them here."[11]

Calvin McDowell grabbed hold of one of the lyncher's guns, and because he would not loosen his grip, a shot was fired into his closed fist. All three men were horribly shot to death, and Calvin McDowell's eyes were gouged out. It was an unwritten rule that to kill a black person in America was not a crime. White mob rule prevailed over the letter of the law.

The news of the lynching shocked African-Americans in Memphis. They gathered together at the grocery store to talk quietly and mourn the deaths of their friends. Upon hearing about the gathering, a white judge told the sheriff to "take a hundred men, go out to the Curve at once, and shoot on sight any Negro who appears to be making trouble."[12]

The news about the judge's order spread throughout the white community, and gangs of men began shooting into any group of blacks whom they saw, as if they were on a hunting trip. One mob ransacked the People's Grocery Company, eating, stealing, and destroying the merchandise.

By the time Ida returned to town from her trip to Mississippi, her dear friend Thomas Moss had already been buried. She wanted to honor his life and protest his death, so she wrote this article, which appeared on the front page of the *Memphis Free Speech and Headlight*:

> The city of Memphis has demonstrated that neither character nor standing avails the Negro if he dares to protect himself against the white man or become his rival. There is nothing we can do about the lynching now, as we are out-numbered and without arms. The white mob could help itself to ammunition without pay, but the order is rigidly enforced against the selling of guns to Negroes. There is therefore only one thing left that we can do; save our money and leave a town which will neither protect our lives and property, nor give us a fair trial in the courts, but takes us out and murders us in cold blood when accused by white persons.[13]

During Ida's lifetime, African-Americans very seldom spoke out so forcefully. It was also unusual for a woman to say the things that Ida said. Ida's strongly worded article was a brave statement.

Crusade for Justice

African-Americans began leaving Memphis by the hundreds. Those who stayed refused to support businesses owned by whites. Local companies such as clothing and furniture and grocery stores depended on African-Americans for their business and lost thousands of dollars. The City Railway Company asked Ida to assure her readers that they would be treated courteously on the streetcars. Ida refused, writing in her diary that "she had never walked so much in her life. . . . Every time word came of people leaving Memphis, we who were left behind rejoiced. Oklahoma was about to be opened up, and scores sold or gave away property, shook Memphis dust off their feet, and went out West as Tom Moss had said for us to do."[1]

Several white newspapers began printing horrible stories about life in Oklahoma to discourage African-Americans from moving there. The papers said that those who left for Oklahoma faced starvation and hostile Native Americans. Ida decided to report on the true conditions in the West and traveled to Guthrie, Oklahoma, Oklahoma City, and other settlements in the territory. Her favorable articles encouraged even more people to move west, including African-Americans who lived in Arkansas, Mississippi, and sections of Tennessee. Although African-Americans still faced racism, the West gave them an opportunity to build their own communities.

Ida also began investigating every lynching that she heard of or read about. She wrote that the deaths of Thomas Moss, Calvin McDowell, and Henry Stewart had "opened my eyes to what lynching really was. An excuse to get rid of Negroes who were acquiring wealth and property and thus keep the race terrorized."[2]

Ida decided that she had to expose lynching to the world and help bring it to an end. She visited Tunica County and Natchez, Mississippi, the sites of two lynchings, to collect the facts and take sworn statements from eyewitnesses. She corresponded with witnesses in other towns where lynchings had occurred. Ida used accounts from white newspapers and let the words of white Southerners speak for themselves to establish the facts about lynching and mob violence. This prevented anyone from saying her accounts were distorted or inaccurate. Ida knew how powerful the written word was.

In 1892, she turned her notes and correspondence into her first published pamphlet about lynching, titled *Southern Horrors*. Ida published two other pamphlets about lynching and mob violence,

A Red Record: Tabulated Statistics and Alleged Causes of Lynching in the United States, 1892, 1893, and 1894, and *Mob Rule in New Orleans*, an account of race riots in New Orleans in 1900. She often used pamphlets to protest against injustice. In 1893, she published a little book called *The Reason Why the Colored American is not in the World's Columbian Exposition* to protest the exclusion of African-Americans from the 1893 World's Fair in Chicago.

Ida was invited to travel to the African Methodist Episcopal General Conference in Philadelphia, and to go to New York to visit T. Thomas Fortune and Jerome B. Peterson, owners of the *New York Age*, a widely circulated African-American newspaper that often reprinted Ida's articles. Before leaving Memphis, Ida wrote the following editorial to be published in the *Memphis Free Speech*:

Eight Negroes lynched since last issue of the *Free Speech*. . . . Nobody in this section believes the old thread-bare lie that Negro men assault white women. If Southern white men are not careful they will over-reach themselves and a conclusion will be reached which will be very damaging to the moral reputation of their women."[3]

The editorial angered many white citizens in Memphis. They felt Ida's article was insulting to white women. They destroyed the offices, furniture, and presses of the *Memphis Free Speech*. Ida's business partner, J. L. Fleming, received a warning from a leading citizen of Memphis and barely escaped being lynched himself. He traveled west, finally

33

settling in Kansas. Ida's friends sent letters informing her that if she ever returned to Memphis she would be killed on sight. The trains and her house were being watched. Ida would never be able to go home to Memphis again.

Ida wrote in her diary:

> I accepted their advice and took a position on the *New York Age* and continued my fight against lynching and lynchers. They had destroyed my paper, in which every dollar I had in the world was invested. They had made me an exile and threatened my life for hinting at the truth. I felt I owed it to myself and my race to tell the whole truth.[4]

Ida received a salary and one-fourth ownership of the *New York Age*. She wrote a full account of her lynching investigations and the destruction of her presses. The *New York Age* published her article on June 7, 1892, in a seven-column spread. Ida named names and cited dates and places for many of the lynchings. It was a bold and shocking article, unlike any other during that time. Ten thousand copies of the paper were printed and distributed around the country and throughout the South. One thousand copies were sold in Memphis alone.

Ida began receiving requests from around the country to give speeches about the horrors of lynching. Her first appearance was before a group of African-American women in New York. After Ida's moving speech, the women banded together to do something about lynching and organized one of

Ida B. Wells, 1893

the first clubs among African-American women in New York.

American women did not have the right to vote, but they began to realize the power they possessed as an organized group to fight against injustices in American society. The club movement spread among women of all races, and Ida helped to form a few of the African-American organizations. Several groups began calling themselves Ida B. Wells Clubs and are still in existence today. Ida's speeches, pamphlets, and newspaper articles helped other women realize that they had the intelligence, the ability, and the obligation to improve life for their families and communities.

Ms. Catherine Impey, a young woman from Somerset, England, heard Ida speak and requested that she visit England, Scotland, and Wales to give speeches about lynching. Ida traveled to Great Britain twice, once in 1893 and a second time in 1894. She stayed several months each time, speaking to hundreds of people about injustice in America. Great Britain was a new experience for Ida. For the first time she received courteous and respectful treatment from white people and their support in her cause to stop lynching. She described her travels in several letters to the *New York Age*. These articles also appeared in other African-American newspapers.

Ida's travels left her very tired. When she returned to America, she decided to make her home in Chicago. There was a growing club movement in that city, and Ida had met a tall, handsome, young widower with two young boys named Ferdinand Lee Barnett. He was an attorney and founder of the city's first African-American newspaper, the *Chicago Conservator*. Ferdinand and Ida were both strong-willed, outspoken, and passionate about the cause of equal rights for African-Americans. Although Ida was usually serious, stubborn, and had few close friends because of her blunt and forceful opinions, Ferdinand was just the opposite. He loved to tease, entertain friends, and tell jokes.

Ferdinand and Ida were married on June 27, 1895. Ida was thirty-three years old. Hundreds of people crowded into the chapel and lined the streets to catch a glimpse of the wedding party.

Many people were happy for Ida, but others, like women's rights activist Susan B. Anthony, believed

Ferdinand L. Barnett Sr.,
Ida's husband
DEPARTMENT OF SPECIAL
COLLECTIONS, THE
UNIVERSITY OF CHICAGO
LIBRARY

her marriage was a mistake and criticized her. Few women during the 1800s had the freedom and power that Ida possessed to make a difference in the lives of women.

Ferdinand realized the importance of Ida's crusade against lynching and recognized her unique talents as a writer and speaker. He wanted her to continue with her work and made it possible for her to do so. He sold Ida his share in *The Chicago Conservator*. She bought the interest of the other partners as well and, for the first time, had full ownership of her own newspaper. In addition, he did not object to her keeping her own name and simply adding Barnett, a bold action for married women to take at that time.

Ida and Ferdinand became the parents of four

children: Charles, Herman, Ida Jr., and Alfreda. Ida pursued the task of being a mother with the same zeal she had devoted to her professional life. "I found that motherhood was a profession by itself, just like schoolteaching and lecturing," she wrote in her diary, "and that once one was launched on such a career, she owed it to herself to become as expert as possible in the practice of her profession."[5] She gave up the paper after Herman's birth in 1897 and did not work outside of the home again until Alfreda was eight years old, although she continued to speak out against injustice and attended meetings in other states, taking her baby along with her.

The Price of Liberty

Ida once said that "the price of liberty is eternal vigilance."[1] She knew that in order to keep the small gains African-Americans had made in their struggle for equal rights, she would have to continue to speak, write, and petition for justice.

Ida was constantly busy reading, writing, and speaking. She continued her duties as president of the Chicago Ida B. Wells Club and her speaking engagements, often bringing her baby, Alfreda, along with her. She was one of the founding members of the National Afro-American Council, the organization that later became the National Association for the Advancement of Colored People (NAACP), and petitioned both Presidents William McKinley and Woodrow Wilson to sign laws that guaranteed just treatment for African-Americans.

Ida's family fully supported her work against injustice. After a lynching in Cairo, Illinois, her husband urged Ida to go investigate. Ida wrote about the incident in her diary:

It was not very convenient for me to be leaving home at that time, and for once, I was quite willing to let them [African-American men] attend to the job. . . . I picked up my baby and took her upstairs to bed. As usual I not only sang her to sleep but put myself to sleep lying there beside her. I was awakened by my oldest child [Charles] who said, "Mother, Pa says it is time to go." "Go where?" I said. "To take the train to Cairo. . . . Mother, if you don't go nobody else will." The next morning all four of my children accompanied my husband and me to the station and saw me start on the journey.[2]

While Ida traveled, Ferdinand often stayed behind to tend to his successful law practice and care for the children. He cooked dinner every night because he enjoyed it and Ida didn't like to, although she did enjoy baking bread.

In 1919, the Barnetts moved to a beautiful home with eight rooms, a ballroom, and a full basement. The Barnetts loved company and often entertained distinguished guests, such as civil rights leader A. Philip Randolph and historian Carter G. Woodson, along with those who were poor, unknown, and less fortunate. The entire family enjoyed playing whist, a card game, and listening to ragtime and opera records on their Victrola. Ida loved the theater and had wanted to become an actress when she was younger, something that was frowned upon by society during her time. She often took her children to the Avenue Theater to see performances by Bert Williams, the Ziegfeld Follies, and actor Abby Mitchell.

Ida B. Wells and her four children in 1909:
Charles, age fourteen; Herman, age twelve;
Ida Jr., age eight; and Alfreda, age five
DEPARTMENT OF SPECIAL COLLECTIONS,
THE UNIVERSITY OF CHICAGO LIBRARY

Although Ida had very little contact with her brothers, Jim Jr. and George, because she didn't approve of their drinking and gambling, she remained close to her sisters. Lillie was married and lived in California. Annie lived in Chicago, where she owned a successful newspaper called *The Searchlight*. The sisters visited often.

Ida continued to get involved in politics and to assist those who needed her help. In 1913, the Barnetts started the Negro Fellowship League in Chicago to improve the plight of African-Americans through better housing, financial assistance, employment counseling, and recreation. For ten years, they ran the league with little financial support from anyone other than themselves. During three of those years, Ida worked as a probation officer. She set up an office in the Negro Fellowship League building to counsel those who were in trouble with the law.

In 1914, Ida became more active in securing women's right to vote and to use the power of the ballot. Suffragettes, as women who wanted to vote were called, were often accused of "trying to take the place of men and wear the trousers," said Ida.[3] Very few African-American women in Chicago had been involved in the suffrage movement before Ida started the Alpha Suffrage Club.

Ida also continued to investigate lynchings, mob violence, and injustice. She played an active part in the committee inquiry into the East Saint Louis riot in 1918, which left 150 people dead and a million dollars' worth of property destroyed.

Ida believed that this disturbance was only the beginning of the city's troubles. In a letter to the *Chicago Tribune*, Ida urged Chicago city leaders to "set the wheels of justice in motion before it was too late." The city took no action, and one of the bloodiest race riots in history erupted shortly afterward.

Ida also arranged small protests of her own. She'd heard that a local department store refused to wait on African-American customers. She visited the store to see if the reports were true. Sure enough, no one would wait on her. Finally, she took a pair of men's

The Barnett family in 1917: *Standing:* Hulette D. Barnett (wife of Albert G. Barnett, Ferdinand's son by his first wife, Margaret Graham Barnett); Herman Kohlsaat Barnett; Ferdinand L. Barnett Jr. (his other son from his first marriage); Ida Jr.; Charles; Alfreda; and Albert G. Barnett *Seated:* Ferdinand L. Barnett Sr.; Beatrice Barnett and Audrey Barnett (Albert's daughters); Ida B. Wells-Barnett *Foreground:* Hulette E. Barnett and Florence B. Barnett (Albert's daughters)

Ida B. Wells-Barnett, 1920 DEPARTMENT OF
SPECIAL COLLECTIONS, THE UNIVERSITY OF
CHICAGO LIBRARY

underwear, draped them over her arm, and walked
toward the door. She was assisted immediately. She
could never tell the story without laughing.

In 1920, Ida was hospitalized for gall bladder
surgery. She spent most all of the following year
recovering from the surgery, but as soon as she was
able to, Ida became active again in Chicago politics.

Because she was one of the founders of the

women's club movement in her city, Ida was very disappointed when she was defeated by educator Mary McLeod Bethune for the presidency of the National Association of Colored Women in 1924. In 1930, Ida lost an election to become an Illinois state senator, but paved the way for other women to pursue a career in politics.

As Ida grew older, she began to feel that her struggles for equality and fairness were being ignored in the history books. After attending a reading at the local Negro History Club in 1928, Ida was disappointed to find no mention about her work as an activist in Carter G. Woodson's book *Negro Makers of History*. Ida decided it was time to write her autobiography and began working on the story of her life in diary form.

"I did more serious thinking from a personal point of view than ever before in my life," Ida wrote. "All at once the realization came to me that I had nothing to show for all those years of toil and labor."[4]

After a brief illness, Ida died suddenly of uremic poisoning, the result of a kidney disease that poisoned her blood, on March 25, 1931, before completing her book. She was sixty-nine years old. She left behind two diaries, one of which became *Crusade for Justice: The Autobiography of Ida B. Wells*, which details Ida's struggles and devotion to the cause of civil rights. Her other diary is titled *The Memphis Diary of Ida B. Wells: An Intimate Portrait of the Activist as a Young Woman,* and chronicles

Ida's years as a young school teacher in Memphis.

After her death, Ida received many of the honors she had wished for during her life. The Ida B. Wells Homes, a federal housing project, was constructed on what is now Martin Luther King Boulevard in Chicago, across from the site of Ida's home, which has been declared an historical landmark. In 1950, the city of Chicago named Ida one of the twenty-five outstanding women in the city's history. On the one hundred and twenty-fifth anniversary of her birth, the Tennessee Historical Commission and the Memphis Community Relations Council placed a historical marker at the site of her *Memphis Free Speech* offices.

The United States Postal Service honored Ida with a postage stamp during Black History Month in 1990. She is also included in several biographical collections about famous women. The details of Ida B. Wells's life and her wonderful achievements are now an important part of modern history books.

Ida left a legacy of public service for the good of all people. She demonstrated the power of the written word for women and men of all races. Her courage to seek as well as speak the truth and her unwavering fight for justice, often as a lone warrior, helped to change the course of American history.

Chronology

1862 Born in Holly Springs, Mississippi on July 16.

1866 Rust University, a high school and industrial school for newly freed slaves is established. Ida attended this school later in her life.

1876 Ida's mother, father, and baby brother die of yellow fever. Ida becomes the head of her family.

1884 Ida is forced off the train on the Memphis-to-Woodstock line. She sues the railroad company, and the court rules in her favor, awarding her five hundred dollars.

1887 The Tennessee Supreme Court reverses the lower court's ruling, and Ida is forced to pay court costs. Ida writes about the case for *The Living Way*, a religious weekly.

1889 Ida buys part of the *Memphis Free Speech and Headlight* and becomes secretary of the Colored Press Association.

1891 The Memphis Board of Education fires Ida because of a critical article she wrote about the schools for African-American children and the conduct of some of their teachers.

1892 Thomas Moss, Calvin McDowell, and Henry Stewart, owners of the People's Grocery Company, are lynched. The article that Ida writes about the incident angers many white townspeople. Mobs destroy her presses and threaten her life. Ida is forced to move to the North.

1893 Ida begins her first speaking tour throughout England, Scotland, and Wales to expose the injustice of lynching.

1895 Ferdinand L. Barnett and Ida B. Wells are married on June 27.

1909 The NAACP is formed. Ida serves on the executive committee.

1913 The Barnetts establish the Negro Fellowship League to assist African-Americans in Chicago. Ida starts the Alpha Suffrage Club to secure women's right to vote, and becomes a probation officer.

1920 Ida undergoes surgery to remove her gall bladder and is slow to recover.

1924 Mary McLeod Bethune defeats Ida for president of the National Association of Colored Women.

1930 Ida loses an election to become a state senator in Illinois.

1931 Ida dies on March 25, after a brief illness.

Endnotes

Chapter 1

1. Alfreda M. Duster, ed., *Crusade for Justice: The Autobiography of Ida B. Wells* (Chicago: University of Chicago Press, 1970, 1972), p. 10.
2. Ibid., p. 15.
3. Ibid., p. 8.
4. Ibid., p. 9.
5. Ibid., p. 11.
6. Ibid.
7. Ibid., p. 12.

Chapter 2

1. Alfreda M. Duster, untitled and unpublished manuscript, *Biography of Ida B. Wells*, p. 5.
2. Ibid., p. 6.
3. Ibid., chapter 2, pp. 1–3.
4. Alfreda M. Duster, ed., *Crusade for Justice: The Autobiography of Ida B. Wells* (Chicago: University of Chicago Press, 1970, 1972), p. 16.

Chapter 3

1. Alfreda M. Duster, untitled and unpublished manuscript, p. 7.

2. Ibid., chapter 3-1, p. 2.
3. Alfreda M. Duster, ed., *Crusade for Justice: The Autobiography of Ida B. Wells* (Chicago: University of Chicago Press, 1970, 1972), p. 19.

Chapter 4

1. Alfreda M. Duster, ed., *Crusade for Justice: The Autobiography of Ida B. Wells* (Chicago: University of Chicago Press, 1970, 1972), p. 19.
2. Miriam DeCosta-Willis, ed., *The Memphis Diary of Ida B. Wells: An Intimate Portrait of the Activist as a Young Woman* (Boston: Beacon Press, 1995), p. 37.
3. Ibid., pp. 21–22.
4. Ibid., p. 23.
5. Ibid., p. 31.
6. Ibid., p. 35.
7. Ibid., p. 36.
8. Ibid., p. 39.
9. Ibid., p. 47.
10. Ibid., p. 49.
11. Ibid., pp. 50–51.
12. Ibid., p. 51.
13. Ibid., p. 52.

Chapter 5

1. Miriam DeCosta-Willis, ed., *The Memphis Diary of Ida B. Wells: An Intimate Portrait of the Activist as a Young Woman* (Boston: Beacon Press, 1995), p. 55.
2. Ibid., p. 64.
3. Ibid., p. 65.
4. Ibid., pp. 62–63.
5. Ibid., pp. 250–51.

Chapter 6

1. Miriam DeCosta-Willis, ed., *The Memphis Diary of Ida B. Wells: An Intimate Portrait of the Activist as a Young Woman* (Boston: Beacon Press, 1995), p. 415.
2. Ibid., pp. 311–12.
3. Ibid., p. 346.
4. Ibid., p. 414.

Further Reading

DeCosta-Willis, Miriam, ed. *The Memphis Diary of Ida B. Wells: An Intimate Portrait of the Activist as a Young Woman*. Boston: Beacon Press, 1995.

Duster, Alfreda M., ed. *Crusade for Justice: The Autobiography of Ida B. Wells*. Chicago: University of Chicago Press, 1970, 1972.

Smith, Jessie Carney, *Epic Lives: One Hundred Black Women Who Made a Difference*. Detroit: Visible Ink Press, 1993.

Index

Page numbers in *italics* refer to photographs.